DAYS
ARE
COMING

*All You Want to
Know about
Mashiach and
the Redemption*

THE REDEMPTION PROCESS

CHAIRMAN
Rabbi Moshe Kotlarsky

PRINCIPAL BENEFACTOR
Mr. George Rohr

EXECUTIVE DIRECTOR
Rabbi Efraim Mintz

EDITOR
Rabbi Ahrele Loschak

ADMINISTRATOR
Rabbi Shlomie Tenenbaum

CURRICULUM TEAM
Rabbi Lazer Gurkow
Rabbi Naftali Silberberg

STEERING COMMITTEE
Rabbi Levi Brook
Rabbi Yosef Raichik
Rabbi Meir Rivkin
Rabbi Zushi Rivkin
Rabbi Yosef Wilhelm

COORDINATOR
Rivki Mockin

The Rohr Jewish Learning Institute
gratefully acknowledges the
pioneering and ongoing support of

George and Pamela Rohr

Since its inception, the Rohr JLI has been
a beneficiary of the vision, generosity,
care, and concern of the Rohr family.

In the merit of the tens of thousands
of hours of Torah study by JLI students
worldwide, may they be blessed with
health, *Yiddishe nachas* from all
their loved ones, and extraordinary
success in all their endeavors.

This series is dedicated
in honor of our dear friends

Yossi and Yael
Michelashvili

May they go from strength to strength
and enjoy good health, happiness,
nachas from their loved ones, and
success in all their endeavors.

Also in memory of his beloved father,
ר' אברהם ב"ר אליהו
on the occasion of his first *yahrtzeit*,
25 Elul 5780.

May the merit of Jews around the world
studying the topic of Redemption in the
Torah bring redemption and merit to
his soul in the world of everlasting life.

May we merit to celebrate the arrival
of the Redemption with Mashiach
speedily in our days.

Contents

Making It Real

A New Consciousness for a New Age

Adapted from a talk of the Rebbe, Shabbat Parshat Balak, 17th of Tamuz, 5751 (1991)

According to all the signs that our sages have foretold of the coming of the Mashiach, it is clear that ours is the last generation of exile and the first generation of the Redemption. We stand at the threshold of the messianic age, at the threshold of the beginning of the Redemption, and very soon, our Redemption will be complete. Thus, the subject of the construction of the Holy Temple must be viewed as one applicable to our present circumstances. It is a discussion that will not only be relevant in the distant future, but at any moment, when the Third Holy Temple—which is already built and waiting in the Heavens—will descend and be manifest on earth.

We are told that studying the laws of the construction of the Holy Temple—like the study of any subject associated with Mashiach and the Redemption—is a means of hastening the coming of this future era. But, in light of the above, it is much more than that: To study these laws is to "live with the times"—to recognize the era of Mashiach as our imminent reality, and to live in that reality. As we reflect on these ideas, our cognitive perception is bound to affect our feelings, and ultimately our deeds and our actions. Thus, our conduct will befit the times in which we find ourselves—at the threshold of Mashiach's coming.

These words are meant as a directive for action. Despite all the recent clamor and excitement about the impending Redemption, it is difficult for people to develop a real awareness that we truly are on the threshold of a new era. The concept is yet to permeate people's consciousness so that the notions of Mashiach and the Redemption become a part of their lives.

How can this be changed? By studying about the concepts of Mashiach and Redemption. The transcendent power of the Torah, which is G-d's wisdom and His will, has the potential to change human character. Thus, by studying these matters, even someone who is only superficially animated by the Redemption idea can begin to live with the idea that Mashiach is coming, and sense that he is coming in the immediate future.

Introduction

Dear Student,

It is with a monumental sense of excitement that we welcome you to the Rohr Jewish Learning Institute's latest course, *Days Are Coming*. Monumental, because this is the first ever course from JLI to present a comprehensive treatment of the subject of *Ge'ulah uMashiach*—the future Redemption of our people from Exile, with the coming of Mashiach.

To many, this might come as a surprise. Chabad's passion for this topic is no secret; the messianic ideal pulses throughout its teachings; the vision of a redeemed world, that of Heaven on earth, lies at the heart of the Lubavitcher Rebbe's life work. The Rebbe spoke of Mashiach incessantly, and repeatedly insisted on the importance of studying the manifold aspects of the future Redemption, as depicted and discussed in traditional Torah sources. As he explained, learning about these subjects is itself a means of hastening the onset of the Redemption. Surely, then, one might have thought that such a course already existed.

In truth, the idea of Mashiach, and its related themes, appears in countless JLI classes and programs, as it is integrated into the rest of the Torah: The purpose of this course is to more fully explicate these vital ideas, to explore why they are such a critical part of Judaism, and to explain just why it is we're so ecstatic about Mashiach. We'll dispel some of the many misconceptions that have accumulated around this much-mischaracterized subject, including one especially important clarification: far from being the exclusive domain of Chabad, or for a few scattered zealots, Mashiach is something for every single Jew to be wildly enthusiastic about—indeed, we always have been. Along with the deep knowledge and familiarity with the subject that you'll gain from the course, we hope it also imparts that same sense of excitement.

After a long and bitter exile, we have been taught that the transformation of the world is just around the corner: the time of our Redemption has arrived. Let us hope and pray that this course—and the increased study and interest in *Ge'ulah uMashiach* it brings—will prove the final step.

1

REDEMPTION: "POOF!" OR PROCESS?

How It Will Be

Miraculousor or Natural? Gradual or Sudden?

TEXT 1

Malachi 3:1

הִנְנִי שֹׁלֵחַ מַלְאָכִי וּפִנָּה דֶרֶךְ לְפָנָי וּפִתְאֹם יָבוֹא אֶל הֵיכָלוֹ
הָאָדוֹן אֲשֶׁר אַתֶּם מְבַקְשִׁים וּמַלְאַךְ הַבְּרִית אֲשֶׁר אַתֶּם
חֲפֵצִים הִנֵּה בָא אָמַר ה' צְבָאוֹת.

"Behold, I send My angel, and he will clear a way before Me. And suddenly, G-d Whom you seek will come to His Temple. And behold! The angel of the covenant, whom you desire, is coming," says G-d of Hosts.

Maimonides, Igeret Teiman

יעמד איש שלא נודע קודם הראותו והאותות והמופתים
שיראו על ידו הן הן הראיות על אמתת יחוסו... בשעה
שיגלה יבהלו כל מלכי ארץ משמעו ויפחדו ותבהל מלכותם
ויתנכלו איך לעמוד כנגדו בחרב או בזולתה כלומר שלא
יוכלו לטעון ולערער עליו ולא יוכלו להכחישו אלא יבהלו
מן המופתים שיראו על ידו וישימו ידם לפיהם שכן אמר
ישעיהו בעת שספר שישמעו המלכים לו אמר "עליו יקפצו
מלכים פיהם כי אשר לא ספר להם ראו ואשר לא שמעו
התבוננו" ואמר שימית כל מי שירצה להמיתו בדברו ולא
יוכל להמלט ולהנצל ממנו שכן אמר "והכה ארץ בשבט פיו
וברוח שפתיו ימית רשע".

The Messiah will be unknown before his coming, but he will prove by means of miracles and wonders that he is the true Messiah. . . . The mere report of his advent will strike terror into the hearts of all the kings of the earth, and their kingdoms will fall as they will be unable to make war or revolt against him. They will neither defame, deny, nor question

---

Rabbi Moshe ben Maimon (Maimonides, Rambam), 1135–1204

Halachist, philosopher, author, and physician. Maimonides was born in Córdoba, Spain. After the conquest of Córdoba by the Almohads, he fled Spain and eventually settled in Cairo, Egypt. There, he became the leader of the Jewish community and served as court physician to the vizier of Egypt. He is most noted for authoring the *Mishneh Torah,* an encyclopedic arrangement of Jewish law; and for his philosophical work, *Guide for the Perplexed.* His rulings on Jewish law are integral to the formation of halachic consensus.

him, for the miracles that he will perform will frighten them into complete silence. Isaiah refers to the submission of the kings to the Messiah in the verse, "Kings shall shut their mouths, for he will be unlike anything they ever saw or heard." He will slay whom he will, none will escape or be saved, as it is written, "And he shall smite the land with the rod of his mouth."

TEXT 3

Jerusalem Talmud, Tractate Berachot 1:1

רבי חייא בר אבא ורבי שמעון בן חלפתא היו מהלכין בבקעת ארבל וראו אילת השחר. אמר לו רבי חייא: כך היא גאולתן של ישראל, בתחילה קמעא קמעא, כל מה שהיא הולכת, היא רבה והולכת. כמו שכתוב: "כי אשב בחשך ה' אור לי".

Rabbi Chiya bar Aba and Rabbi Shimon ben Chalafta were walking in the valley of Arbel, and they witnessed the advent of dawn. Rabbi Chiya told Rabbi Shimon, "So will be the redemption of the Jewish people: at first, it will be a trickle,

---

Jerusalem Talmud

A commentary to the Mishnah, compiled during the 4th and 5th centuries. The Jerusalem Talmud predates its Babylonian counterpart by 100 years and is written in both Hebrew and Aramaic. While the Babylonian Talmud is the most authoritative source for Jewish law, the Jerusalem Talmud remains an invaluable source for the spiritual, intellectual, ethical, historical, and legal traditions of Judaism.

and as it continues, it will gain steam and expand, as it is stated, 'Though I will sit in darkness, G-d is a light to me.'"

TEXT 4

Maimonides, Mishneh Torah, *Laws of Kings and Wars 11:3, 12:1–2*

אל יעלה על דעתך שהמלך המשיח צריך לעשות אותות ומופתים ומחדש דברים בעולם או מחיה מתים וכיוצא בדברים אלו אין הדבר כך...

אל יעלה על הלב שבימות המשיח יבטל דבר ממנהגו של עולם או יהיה שם חידוש במעשה בראשית, אלא עולם כמנהגו נוהג... אמרו חכמים אין בין העולם הזה לימות המשיח אלא שיעבוד מלכיות בלבד.

One should not presume that the messianic king must work miracles and wonders, bring about new phenomena in the world, resurrect the dead, or perform other similar deeds. This is not the case. . . . Do not presume that in the messianic age any facet of the world's nature will change or there will be innovations in the work of Creation. Rather, the world will continue according to its pattern. . . .

Our sages taught, "There will be no difference between the current age and the messianic era except our emancipation from subjugation to the gentile kingdoms."

The Worthy/ Unworthy Binary

TEXT 5

Talmud, Tractate Sanhedrin 98a

אמר רבי אלכסנדרי, רבי יהושע בן לוי רמי כתיב "בעתה"
וכתיב "אחישנה"?

זכו אחישנה; לא זכו בעתה.

Rabbi Alexandri says, "Rabbi Yehoshua ben Levi raises a contradiction. [The verse, "I, G-d, in its time, I will hasten it,"] reads, "in its time," [indicating that there is a designated

---

Babylonian Talmud

A literary work of monumental proportions that draws upon the legal, spiritual, intellectual, ethical, and historical traditions of Judaism. The 37 tractates of the Babylonian Talmud contain the teachings of the Jewish sages from the period after the destruction of the 2nd Temple through the 5th century CE. It has served as the primary vehicle for the transmission of the Oral Law and the education of Jews over the centuries; it is the entry point for all subsequent legal, ethical, and theological Jewish scholarship.

time for the Redemption,] and it reads, "I will hasten it," [indicating that there is no set time for the Redemption]."

[Rabbi Alexandri explains,] "If they merit, I will hasten [the coming of the Messiah]. If they do not merit, [Messiah will come] in its [designated] time."

TEXT 6

Rabbi Chaim ibn Atar, Or Hachayim, *Numbers 24:16*

שאם תהיה הגאולה באמצעות זכות ישראל יהיה הדבר מופלא במעלה ויתגלה הגואל ישראל מן השמים במופת ואות כאמור בספר הזוהר, מה שאין כן כשתהיה הגאולה מצד הקץ ואין ישראל ראויים לה תהיה באופן אחר, ועליה נאמר שהגואל יבא "עני ורוכב על חמור".

והוא מה שאמר כאן כנגד גאולת אחישנה שהיא באמצעות זכות ישראל... וכנגד גאולת בעתה... שיקום שבט אחד מישראל כדרך הקמים בעולם דרך טבע.

Rabbi Chaim ibn Atar (*Or Hachayim*), 1696–1743

Biblical exegete, kabbalist, and Talmudist. Rabbi Atar, born in Meknes, Morocco, was a prominent member of the Moroccan rabbinate and later immigrated to the Land of Israel. He is most famous for his *Or Hachayim,* a popular commentary on the Torah. The famed Jewish historian and bibliophile Rabbi Chaim Yosef David Azulai was among his most notable disciples.

If the Redemption will arrive through the merits of the Jewish people, it will be wondrous: the redeemer will appear miraculously from the heavens. By contrast, if the Jews are unworthy, and the Redemption comes only because the clock ran out, it will be different, regarding which the Talmud states the redeemer will "arrive as a pauper riding on a donkey."

The prophecy that the Redemption will be "hastened" will occur if the Jewish people will be worthy. . . . Regarding a Redemption in "the set time" . . . the verse states that a "Ruler will arise in Israel" naturally, as do all rulers in this world.

The Qualities of Achishenah

TEXT 7

Rabbi Chaim Yeshaya Halbersberg,
Kets Hapla'ot, *p. 7*

וכל אלו השינוים דאיתא בגמרא ומדרשים שיהיה
קודם ביאת משיח, כוונתם דכל זה צריך להיות קודם
הקץ דבעתה... ולכן היו מצפים משה רבינו ע"ה וכל
הצדיקים אחריו להקץ דאחישנה כדי שיהיה הכל במהרה
בתכלית הטובה.

Rabbi Chaim Yeshaya Halbersberg, 1848–1910

Halachic authority and Chasidic rebbe. Rabbi Halbersberg frequented the Chasidic courts of Ostrowiec, Trisk, and Lublin. He served as rabbi in various cities in Poland, eventually immigrating to Jerusalem. He authored numerous books, and is best known for *Misgeret Hashulchan*, his commentary and glosses on the *Kitsur Shulchan Aruch*—the acclaimed *"Abridged Code of Jewish Law"* authored by Rabbi Shlomo Ganzfried.

When the Talmud and Midrash speak of the many changes that will occur prior to Mashiach's arrival, the context is that such events must occur only prior to a Redemption that comes "in the designated time." . . . Thus, Moses and all subsequent sages anticipated a Redemption of achishenah, so that everything can be in the best possible manner.

TEXT 8

The Rebbe, Rabbi Menachem Mendel Schneerson,
Torat Menachem 5730:3 (60), pp. 6–7

דהנה יש סדר העבודה דבעתה שעל זה נאמר "קץ שם
לחושך", שיש קצבה מצד הטבע והבריאה כמה שיומשך
להם, וככלות הזמן יאבדו לגמרי ולא ישאר מהם מאומה,
וכמו שכתוב "את רוח הטומאה אעביר מן הארץ".
אמנם סדר זה הוא כאשר ישראל לא זכו ח"ו לפעול
ענין זה על ידי עבודתם בענין הבירורים, שאז נעשה קץ
הימים... מצד עצמה.

Rabbi Menachem Mendel Schneerson, 1902–1994

The towering Jewish leader of the 20th century, known as "the Lubavitcher Rebbe," or simply as "the Rebbe." Born in southern Ukraine, the Rebbe escaped Nazi-occupied Europe, arriving in the U.S. in June 1941. The Rebbe inspired and guided the revival of traditional Judaism after the European devastation, impacting virtually every Jewish community the world over. The Rebbe often emphasized that the performance of just one additional good deed could usher in the era of Mashiach. The Rebbe's scholarly talks and writings have been printed in more than 200 volumes.

אבל כאשר זכו ישראל בעבודת הבירורים, אזי תהיה הגאולה קודם הזמן הקצוב כשיש עדיין מציאות החושך כו', הנה גם שם נעשה ענין הבירור כו'... שזוהי המעלה באחישנה על בעתה.

There is, indeed, a paradigm about which the verse states, "G-d set a date for evil": Creation itself dictates that evil only has a certain timespan, after which it will expire and disappear without a trace, as the verse states, "And I will remove the spirit of veil from the world." However, this paradigm is only reserved for a situation in which the Jewish people haven't managed to make such a reality happen with their own transformative work. Then, indeed, the end of days happens . . . on its own.

However, if the Jews are so worthy and transform the world, the Redemption will arrive prior to its allotted time, for though the clock will not yet have run out on evil, the Jews will have managed to banish it with their transformative work. . . .

This, then, is the true quality of achishenah *over* be'itah: *it transforms even the darkest of evils.*

It Can Happen Any Day!

TEXT 9

The Rebbe, Rabbi Menachem Mendel Schneerson, Sefer Hasichot 5751:2, p. 793

וואס על פי זה האט מען אויך אן ענטפער אויף דער שאלה וואס מ'פרעגט אויף דעם וואס מ'רעדט לאחרונה אז די גאולה קומט תיכף ומיד ממש – לכאורה:

ווי קען דאס אזוי גלאטיק דורכגיין און מצליח זיין; ווי וועלן די בני בית זיך אפרופען אויף דעם, און וואס וועט די וועלט זאגן אויף דעם?!

איז דער ענטפער אז אויב די עניני הגאולה וואלטן געווען א חידוש וואלט אפשר געוווען אן ארט אויף דער שאלה; ווייבאלד אבער אז די גאולה איז ניט קיין חידוש דבר, נאר כל עניני הגאולה האבן זיך שוין אנגעהויבן און זיינען שוין נמשך ונתקבל געוווארן אין עולם הזה הגשמי התחתון

We now have an answer to all the chatter about our recent
hype about Mashiach's imminent arrival. After all, how will
such hype be received at home? What will Main Street think
about such talk?

The answer is: If the elements of Redemption were completely
foreign, it would, indeed, be a tough sell. However, because
they are not foreign at all, and in fact, much of it is already
underway in our very material present-day reality, an imminent Redemption will not be a surprise at all!

TEXT 10

The Rebbe, Rabbi Menachem Mendel Schneerson,
Sefer Hasichot 5752, p. 363; 5751:1, p. 73

בימים אלו מחליטים ומכריזים ראשי מדינות בעולם על
דבר צמצום וביטול כלי נשק והוספה בהענינים הדרושים
לקיום כלכלת המדינה והעולם כולו - תוכן היעוד "וכתתו
חרבותם לאתים", שבירת כלי המלחמה לעשות מהם כלים
לעבודת האדמה, "ארץ ממנה יצא לחם" - הרי זה סימן
ברור על התחלת קיומו של יעוד זה בגאולה האמיתית
והשלימה על ידי משיח צדקנו...

In these times, heads of state the world over have decided to reduce their weapons capacity and invest in economic, peaceful measures. This is, after all, what the prophet promises, that "They will beat their swords into plowshares"—dismantling weapons and fashioning them into tools to work the ground to produce bread. We have a clear sign that the signs of the ultimate Redemption are beginning to blossom. . . .

Many great and mighty countries have reformed and established noble governments, grounded in just and fair laws. This, too, is a foretaste of the overall reform and peace that Mashiach will bring to the world. Another realization of this promise is the world's attitude to the Jewish people, as we have been granted religious freedom.

2

GOG AND MAGOG

Turbulent, Terrible…
and Terrific!

The
Basics

TEXT 1

Ezekiel 38:1–3, 10–12, 18, 22–23

וַיְהִי דְבַר ה' אֵלַי לֵאמֹר:

בֶּן אָדָם שִׂים פָּנֶיךָ אֶל גּוֹג אֶרֶץ הַמָּגוֹג נְשִׂיא רֹאשׁ מֶשֶׁךְ וְתֻבָל וְהִנָּבֵא עָלָיו:

וְאָמַרְתָּ כֹּה אָמַר אֲדֹנָ-י ה' הִנְנִי אֵלֶיךָ גּוֹג נְשִׂיא רֹאשׁ מֶשֶׁךְ וְתֻבָל:...

כֹּה אָמַר אֲדֹנָ-י ה' וְהָיָה בַּיּוֹם הַהוּא יַעֲלוּ דְבָרִים עַל לְבָבֶךָ וְחָשַׁבְתָּ מַחֲשֶׁבֶת רָעָה:

וְאָמַרְתָּ אֶעֱלֶה עַל אֶרֶץ פְּרָזוֹת אָבוֹא הַשֹּׁקְטִים יֹשְׁבֵי לָבֶטַח כֻּלָּם יֹשְׁבִים בְּאֵין חוֹמָה וּבְרִיחַ וּדְלָתַיִם אֵין לָהֶם:

לִשְׁלֹל שָׁלָל וְלָבֹז בַּז לְהָשִׁיב יָדְךָ עַל חֳרָבוֹת נוֹשָׁבֹת וְאֶל עַם מְאֻסָּף מִגּוֹיִם עֹשֶׂה מִקְנֶה וְקִנְיָן יֹשְׁבֵי עַל טַבּוּר הָאָרֶץ:...

וְהָיָה בַּיּוֹם הַהוּא בְּיוֹם בּוֹא גוֹג עַל אַדְמַת יִשְׂרָאֵל נְאֻם אֲדֹנָ-י ה' תַּעֲלֶה חֲמָתִי בְּאַפִּי:...

וְנִשְׁפַּטְתִּי אִתּוֹ בְּדֶבֶר וּבְדָם וְגֶשֶׁם שׁוֹטֵף וְאַבְנֵי אֶלְגָּבִישׁ אֵשׁ וְגָפְרִית אַמְטִיר עָלָיו וְעַל אֲגַפָּיו וְעַל עַמִּים רַבִּים אֲשֶׁר אִתּוֹ:

וְהִתְגַּדִּלְתִּי וְהִתְקַדִּשְׁתִּי וְנוֹדַעְתִּי לְעֵינֵי גּוֹיִם רַבִּים וְיָדְעוּ כִּי אֲנִי ה':

Then the word of G-d came to me, saying:

Son of man, set your face toward Gog, [toward] the land of Magog, the prince, the head of Meshech and Tubal, and prophesy concerning him.

And you shall say, "So said the L-rd G-d, 'Behold, I am against you, Gog, the prince, the head of Meshech and Tubal. . . .'

"So said the L-rd G-d, 'It will come to pass on that day that words will enter your heart and you will think a thought of evil.'"

And you will say, "I shall ascend upon a land of open cities; I shall come upon the tranquil, who dwell securely; all of them living without a wall, and they have no bars or doors.

"To take spoil and to plunder loot, to return your hand upon the resettled ruins and to a people gathered from nations, acquiring livestock and possessions, dwelling on the navel of the earth. . . ."

And it will come to pass on that day, when Gog comes against the Land of Israel, declares the L-rd G-d that My blazing indignation will flame in My nostrils. . . .

And I will judge against him with pestilence and with blood, and rain bringing floods, and great hailstones, fire, and brimstone will I rain down upon him and upon his hordes and upon the many peoples that are with him.

And I will reveal Myself in My greatness and in My holiness and will be recognized in the eyes of many nations, and they will know that I am G-d.

TEXT 2

Rabbi Meir Leibush Wisser,
Pirush HaMalbim, *Ezekiel 39:8*

מפני שהיום הזה מיועד סתום וחתום ולא הודיעו ה' לשום
נביא וחוזה ולבא לפומא לא גליא, ועדיין אינו במציאות
בעולם החזיון בפועל, רק בעת שיבא הדבר ויהיה אז
הוא היום אשר דברתי אז יבא אל מציאות הדבור ואז
יתרשם בפועל.

Rabbi Meir Leibush Wisser (Malbim), 1809–1879

Rabbi, Hebrew grammarian, and Bible commentator. Born in Ukraine, Rabbi Wisser served as rabbi in several prestigious communities across Europe. His fame reached as far as the Jewish community of New York, which offered him the position of first chief rabbi of the city, an offer he rejected. He is best known for his commentary to the entire Bible, which was unprecedented in its scope and thoroughness. He placed great emphasis on explaining the precise meaning of every word in the Bible.

The designated day is hidden and closed, for G-d did not reveal it to any prophet, nor has anyone ever uttered it. The vision has not yet occurred in this world. Only when the events happen and the spoken day will arrive, then matters will be clear.

TEXT 3

Rabbi Meir Leibush Wisser, Ibid. 38:17

כי שם גוג ושם מגוג כבר ישכח בימים ההם עד שלא ידעו
כלל מי היא האומה שנקראת בפי הנביא מגוג ושם מלכה
גוג, רק אז כשיבוא על הארץ ויתקיימו דברי הנביא, אז ידעו
שזה הוא המלך גוג שניבא עליו.

The names "Gog" and "Magog" have already been forgotten, and we no longer have any idea which nation is the one the prophet named "Magog," whose king is named "Gog." When they will actually come and the prophet's words realized, then we will know that this is the Gog of which the prophet spoke.

An Epic Battle

TEXT 4

Midrash, Yalkut Shimoni, *Vayikra 23:653*

לעתיד לבוא עתידין אומות העולם להכנס על ארץ ישראל
ולעשות מלחמה עמהם, ומה הקדוש ברוך הוא עושה? יוצא
ונלחם עם הגויים ...ומסכך על ראשם של ישראל, שנאמר
סכותה לראשי ביום נשק, אמר רבי שמואל בר נחמן ביום
שישקו שני עולמות זה לזה.

---

*In future times, the nations will gather up against Israel
and wage war. What will G-d do? He will go out and battle*

Yalkut Shimoni

A Midrash that covers the entire biblical text. Its material is collected from
all over rabbinic literature, including the Babylonian and Jerusalem Talmuds
and various ancient Midrashic texts. It contains several passages from
Midrashim that have been lost, as well as different versions of existing
Midrashim. It is unclear when and by whom this Midrash was redacted.

them. . . . He will protect the Jews' heads, as the verse states, "You shall protect my head on the day of battle (nashek)." Rabbi Shmuel bar Nachman said, "This is a reference to the day when the two worlds will meet (yashku) one another."

What's the Point?

TEXT 5

Rabbi Yehudah Lowe, Netsach Yisrael ch. *35*

כל הויה חדשה הוא הפסד הויה הראשונה, ולפיכך הוא
הגורם שיהיה העדר הויה בעולם קודם שיתגלה המשיח, עד
שיהיה כאן הפסד הויה הראשונה ואז יתחיל ההויה החדשה.

All new creation comes after the destruction of the old reality.
Thus, there must be something that causes utter destruction
of the current reality prior to Mashiach's revelation. It must

---

Rabbi Yehudah Lowe (Maharal of Prague), 1525–1609

Talmudist and philosopher. Maharal rose to prominence as leader of the
famed Jewish community of Prague. He is the author of more than a dozen
works of original philosophic thought, including *Tiferet Yisrael* and *Netsach
Yisrael*. He also authored *Gur Aryeh,* a supercommentary to Rashi's biblical
commentary; and a commentary on the nonlegal passages of the Talmud.
He is buried in the Old Jewish Cemetery of Prague.

be completely removed, and only then can the new reality settle in.

TEXT 6

Rabbi Yehudah Lowe, Ibid. ch. 38

וזהו עניין מלחמת גוג ומגוג שתהיה לעתיד עם המלך המשיח, שכל העובדי כוכבים ומזלות אשר הם הריבוי, יתחברו יחד על המלך המשיח שהוא מלך ישראל לאומה יחידה ... אם כן מלחמת גוג ומגוג הוא על השם יתברך נחשב בפרט, כי הוא יתברך אחדות ישראל ... לימות במשיח שאז יהיה הוא יתברך אחד ושמו אחד לגמרי, אז יתנגדו העובדי כוכבים ומזלות ... שלא יהיה הוא יתברך מולך עליהם...

לכח מעלת משיח בן דוד לא יהיה לו הפסק. ואז יהיו גוים נחלתו ואחוזתו אפסי ארץ, כי יתגבר משיח בן דוד על העכו"ם ויסלק כח העובדי כוכבים ומזלות ועמהם מסתלק היצר הרע ... והתבאר לך מזה כי מלחמה זאת של גוג ומגוג להסיר חסרון עולם הזה ולכך יוסר אז היצר הרע.

This, then, is the idea of the wars of Gog and Magog that are destined to be with Mashiach. All the nations—representing division—will band together to battle Mashiach, who is the king of the one unified nation of the Jews. . . . Thus, the battle of Gog and Magog is really against G-d, for He is the One that unites Israel. . . . In the messianic era, when G-d and

His name will be completely one, the forces of evil will rise up and oppose G-d's rule. . . .

The force of Mashiach's kingdom is, by definition, unstoppable, and so, he will rule over all nations, for Mashiach will overpower them and remove the powers of evil and eradicate the yetser hara *[evil inclination]. . . .*

It emerges from all the above that the war of Gog and Magog is to remove the deficiency of this world, and then, the yetser hara *will be removed as well.*

TEXT 7

Rabbi Shne'ur Zalman of Liadi,
Maamarim Ketsarim, *pp. 552–553*

להבין עניו גלות הזה שנתארך מאד... כי בימי בית ראשון כשהיו הנביאים מוכיחים לא היו כופרים בחטאיהם והיה הרע שלהם בהתגלות אלא היו אומרים בפירוש שרוצים בעבודה זרה וכדומה שאז היה חיות רב להעומת זה לעמוד כו' עד שבטלוהו אנשי כנסת הגדולה כו', לכן היה בנקל להם לחזור בתשובה, כי אין צריך לשהות זמן רב – או זה יצליח, או זה כו'.

Rabbi Shne'ur Zalman of Liadi (Alter Rebbe), 1745–1812

Chasidic rebbe, halachic authority, and founder of the Chabad movement. The Alter Rebbe was born in Liozna, Belarus, and was among the principal students of the Magid of Mezeritch. His numerous works include the *Tanya*, an early classic containing the fundamentals of Chabad Chasidism; and *Shulchan Aruch HaRav*, an expanded and reworked code of Jewish law.

אבל גלות הזה הוא בחינת לבן הארמי שדר יעקב אצלו
עשרים שנה עד שהכניעו מפני כי הוא גניבת דעת ורמאות,
דהיינו באם שהיה יודע כל אחד ואחד מישראל שבעבירה
אחת מעבירות הוא נפרד מכל ישראל ואין לו חלק באלקי
ישראל, בוודאי לא היה עושה זה,רק הוא מוצא לו היתר
לומר אעפ"כ אני ישראל ונמצא הרע אצלו בהסתר
וברמאות שהיצה"ר גונב דעתו שאינו יודע כי ברע הוא כו'
ולבו יכול לשהות זמן רב עד שיפטור ממנו וזהו עם לבן
גרתי כו' היה וצריך לדור אצלו זמן רב, אבל אחר כך כשיצא
עשו לקראתו שהוא מלחמת גוג ומגוג, שהיצר הרע עומד
בפרהסיא ובהתגלות במהרה ינצחו.

Why is this current exile so long? . . .

During the times of the First Temple, when the prophets would rebuke the Jews they would not deny their wrongdoing; their perjury was out in the open, and they would say outright that they wished to serve idols, etc. At that time, the evil forces were very strong, up until the point when the Men of the Great Assembly eradicated it. Thus, it was easier for them to repent, for there isn't much to wait for—either this one wins, or the other. . . .

By contrast, this current exile is represented by Laban the Aramean, with whom Jacob lived for twenty years until he was able to subdue him—such a long time because Laban was a trickster and swindler. In other words, if a Jew would know that with one sin he excises himself from the Jewish people and from G-d, he would never commit a sin! But he fabricates excuses, convincing himself that his sins have no impact.

It turns out that the evil is hidden and cunning; the yetser hara *[evil inclination] fools him to the extent that he doesn't even realizes it's bad. Thus, it takes a long time to weed this out.*

And so, Jacob had to live with Laban for so long. However, later, when Esau will re-greet him in the future showdown with Gog and Magog, when the yetser hara *will stand in open defiance, it will be speedily eradicated.*

TEXT 8

Rabbi Shmuel Borenstein, Shem MiShmuel *5677,*
Vayigash, p. 298

קבלה בידנו מרבותינו הקדושים, שמעתה נפטרנו
ממלחמות גוג ומגוג ואחר קיבוץ גליות ישבו ישראל
במנוחה על אדמתם לעולם... שהאריכות הזמן השלים
לקישוי השעבוד ורעות רבות וצרות שהיה מעותד לבוא
על שונאי ישראל, על כן באשר אריכות הזמן השלים...
וכשיתקבץ הגליות לא נצטרך עוד לשום מירוק.

*We have a tradition from our holy teachers that by now, we
have been spared from the wars of Gog and Magog. After the
Jews will be gathered together, they will peacefully settle the
Land. . . . The protracted time in exile has made up for the
intense suffering and calamities that were destined to befall
the Jewish people in the future. Inasmuch as the current exile
has lasted so long . . . when the ingathering will take place,
the Jews will not need any more cleansing.*

Rabbi Shmuel Borenstein, 1855–1926

Chasidic Rebbe. Rabbi Borenstein was born in Poland into a distinguished
rabbinic family. His father and primary teacher, Rabbi Avraham—known
by the title of his halachic responsa *Avnei Nezer*—was the first Rebbe of
Sochatchov, and his maternal grandfather was Rabbi Menachem Mendel
Morgenstern, the Rebbe of Kotzk. In 1910, Rabbi Shmuel succeeded his
father as Rebbe of Sochatchov and established a yeshiva there. He is best
known for the collection of his Chasidic sermons, *Shem MiShmuel*, which
has gained wide popularity.

TEXT 9

The Rebbe, Rabbi Menachem Mendel Schneerson,
Torat Menachem 38 (5724:1), p. 53

מלחמת גוג ומגוג בעבודת האדם - עניינה הוא המלחמה עם
ז' המדות רעות, כל אחת כפי שהיא כלולה מעשר (שבעים
אומות) שהרי צריך לברר כל מדה לכל פרטי' ובכל ענפי'...
לבררם ולזככם ולפעול בהם שיתעלו לבחי' "הרי ישראל"
שהכוונה בזה היא להרי ירושלים - שלימות היראה...

ועניין זה הוא בכחו של כאו"א מישראל...

ועי"ז שכאו"א מישראל פועל עניין זה בעצמו - הנה "גם
את העולם נתן בלבם" שפועל גם את נצחון המלחמה בכל
שבעים האומות במלחמת גוג ומגוג כפשוטה.

וזהו הטעם שהודיעו לנו אודות מלחמת גוג ומגוג שתהי' עם
כל האומות יחד ושאר פרטי עניני המלחמה כו' - כדי שנדע
מהי העבודה המוטלת עלינו ועי"י נצחון המלחמה בעבודה
הרוחנית נפעל גם נצחון המלחמה כפשוטה, בגאולה
העתידה והשלימה (שכל עניני הגאולה תלויים "במעשינו

Rabbi Menachem Mendel Schneerson, 1902–1994

The towering Jewish leader of the 20th century, known as "the Lubavitcher Rebbe," or simply as "the Rebbe." Born in southern Ukraine, the Rebbe escaped Nazi-occupied Europe, arriving in the U.S. in June 1941. The Rebbe inspired and guided the revival of traditional Judaism after the European devastation, impacting virtually every Jewish community the world over. The Rebbe often emphasized that the performance of just one additional good deed could usher in the era of Mashiach. The Rebbe's scholarly talks and writings have been printed in more than 200 volumes.

The battle of Gog and Magog in a personal sense represents every individual's struggle with their seven negative impulses, each one as it is comprised of ten different strains (represented in the seventy nations). After all, one must work with every emotion and all of its strains . . . namely, to transform them and raise them up to the "hills of Jerusalem," namely the ultimate sense of fearing G-d.

Every Jew is capable of doing so. . . .

When, indeed, every Jews does so, then—based on the notion that "also the world He put into their hearts"—the actions of the individual Jew have a global effect: it generates victory over the seventy nations in the literal battle of Gog and Magog.

This, then, is the reason why we are told about the battle of Gog and Magog and all the nations, with all the other details, etc.—so that we can be informed as to what we ought to do now. Inasmuch as the future Redemption is directly hinged upon our work in exile, we now know that our personal spiritual victories are the pathway to the global literal victory with Mashiach. May he come soon and lead us upright to our Promised Land!

3

ELIJAH THE
PROPHET PART I

Harbinger of the Redemption

SECTION ONE

Who Is Elijah?

TEXT 1

II Kings 2:8–12

וַיִּקַּח אֵלִיָּהוּ אֶת אַדַּרְתּוֹ וַיִּגְלֹם וַיַּכֶּה אֶת הַמַּיִם וַיֵּחָצוּ הֵנָּה
וָהֵנָּה וַיַּעַבְרוּ שְׁנֵיהֶם בֶּחָרָבָה:

וַיְהִי כְעָבְרָם וְאֵלִיָּהוּ אָמַר אֶל אֱלִישָׁע שְׁאַל מָה אֶעֱשֶׂה
לָךְ בְּטֶרֶם אֶלָּקַח מֵעִמָּךְ וַיֹּאמֶר אֱלִישָׁע וִיהִי נָא פִּי שְׁנַיִם
בְּרוּחֲךָ אֵלָי:

וַיֹּאמֶר הִקְשִׁיתָ לִשְׁאוֹל אִם תִּרְאֶה אֹתִי לֻקָּח מֵאִתָּךְ יְהִי לְךָ כֵן
וְאִם אַיִן לֹא יִהְיֶה:

וַיְהִי הֵמָּה הֹלְכִים הָלוֹךְ וְדַבֵּר וְהִנֵּה רֶכֶב אֵשׁ וְסוּסֵי אֵשׁ וַיַּפְרִדוּ
בֵּין שְׁנֵיהֶם וַיַּעַל אֵלִיָּהוּ בַּסְעָרָה הַשָּׁמָיִם:

וֶאֱלִישָׁע רֹאֶה וְהוּא מְצַעֵק אָבִי אָבִי רֶכֶב יִשְׂרָאֵל וּפָרָשָׁיו וְלֹא
רָאָהוּ עוֹד וַיַּחֲזֵק בִּבְגָדָיו וַיִּקְרָעֵם לִשְׁנַיִם קְרָעִים:

And Elijah took his mantle and rolled it up, and struck the water, and it divided to this side and to that side; and they both crossed on dry land.

And it was when they crossed that Elijah said to Elisha, "Ask what I shall do for you, while I am not yet taken away from you."

And Elisha said, "Please let there be a double portion of your spirit on me."

And he said, "You have made a difficult request. If you see me taken from you, it will be so to you, and if not, it will not be."

And it was that they were going, walking and talking, and behold, a fiery chariot and fiery horses, and they separated them both. And Elijah ascended to Heaven in a whirlwind.

And Elisha saw, and he was crying, "My father! My father! The chariots of Israel and their riders!" And he saw him no longer. Now he took hold of his garments and rent them in two pieces.

Elijah Today

TEXT 2

Midrash, Pirkei Rabbi Eliezer, *ch. 28*

נמלט ועמד אליהו ז"ל וברח לו להר חורב, שנאמר: "ויקם
ויאכל וישתה", ושם נגלה לו הקדוש ברוך הוא. אמר לו:
"מה לך פה אליהו"? "קנא קנאתי". אמר לו: לעולם אתה
מקנא, קנאת בשטים על גלוי עריות, שנאמר "פנחס בן
אלעזר בן אהרן הכהן", וכאן קנאת.

---

*Elijah escaped and fled to Mount Horeb, as the verse states,
"And he got up, and ate and drank." There, G-d revealed*

Pirkei Rabbi Eliezer

A Midrash bearing the name of Rabbi Eliezer ben Hyrcanus, a prominent
rabbinic sage living during the first and second centuries. Pirkei Rabbi
Eliezer commences with the story of the early days of Rabbi Eliezer's life
and then chronologically narrates and expounds upon events from the
Creation until the middle of the journeys of the Children of Israel in the
wilderness.

Himself to Elijah. G-d asked him, "What are you doing here, Elijah?"

"I have been zealous for G-d."

"You have always been zealous. You were zealous in Shitim to stand up to promiscuity, as the verse states, 'Pinchas the son of Elazar, the son of Aaron the Priest.' And here, too, you have been zealous."

TEXT 3

Rabbi Yosef Caro, Shulchan Aruch, Yoreh De'ah *265:11*

נוהגין לעשות כסא לאליהו שנקרא מלאך הברית וכשמניחו יאמר בפיו שהוא כסא אליהו.

It is customary to set aside a chair for Elijah, the angel of brit milah. *When the baby is placed on the chair, we proclaim, "This is the chair of Elijah."*

Rabbi Yosef Caro (Maran, *Beit Yosef*), 1488–1575

Halachic authority and author. Rabbi Caro was born in Spain but was forced to flee during the Expulsion in 1492 and eventually settled in Safed, Israel. He authored many works, including the *Beit Yosef, Kesef Mishneh*, and a mystical work, *Magid Meisharim*. Rabbi Caro's magnum opus, the Shulchan Aruch (Code of Jewish Law), has been universally accepted as the basis for modern Jewish law.

TEXT 4

Rabbi Shneur Zalman of Liadi,
Shulchan Aruch HaRav 480:5

בקצת מקומות נוהגין שלא לנעול החדרים שישנים שם
בליל פסח כי הוא ליל ליל שמורים לכל בני ישראל לדורותם
להוציאם מגלות הזה ואם יבא אליהו ימצא פתח פתוח
ונצא לקראתו במהרה ואנו מאמינים בזה ויש באמונה זו
שכר גדול ובמקומות שמצויין גנבים אין לסמוך על הנס.

ונוהגין במדינות אלו למזוג כוס אחד יותר מהמסובין וקורין
אותו כוס של אליהו הנביא.

There is a custom in certain communities not to lock the
doors of the rooms in which they sleep on the seder night,
for it is the "Guardian Night" for all Israel for all time. It is a
night for redemption from this exile, and when Elijah comes,
he should find an open door. We will go out to greet him very
soon. We believe this, and there is great reward to this belief.
Of course, in places where there are many thieves, we do not
rely on miracles.

The custom in these communities is to pour an extra cup,
and we call it "Elijah the Prophet's Cup."

Rabbi Shne'ur Zalman of Liadi (Alter Rebbe), 1745–1812

Chasidic rebbe, halachic authority, and founder of the Chabad movement.
The Alter Rebbe was born in Liozna, Belarus, and was among the principal
students of the Magid of Mezeritch. His numerous works include the *Tanya,*
an early classic containing the fundamentals of Chabad Chasidism; and
Shulchan Aruch HaRav, an expanded and reworked code of Jewish law.

Rabbi Yehudah Loew, Haggadah shel Pesach,
Divrei Negidim *to* Shfoch Chamatcha

והנראה לי בטעמא דהך מנהגא שכיון שההלל נרצה בא
לעורר רחמים ורצון העליון עליה שנזכה להיות נרצה לפני
הקדוש ברוך הוא והוא יתרצה אתנו ויגאלנו בגאולה שלמה,
לפיכך אנו מחויבים להודיע לבנינו ולפרסם מה שקבלה
בידינו מן הנביאים שטרם שיבא הגואל צדק יקדים אליהו
הנביא לבוא לבשר לנו הגאולה...

והנה בא פירושו מקודם ביאת האדון המשיח אל היכלו,
ועל כן זה האות שהוא הוא הגואל צדק... והרי זה יסוד אמת
ועיקר גדול לאמונת ביאת המשיח שאנו מצפים עליו למען
לא נפול ברשת איזו משיח שקר. ולפיכך נוהגין כאן לפתוח
הדלת לכבודו של אליהו הנביא וגם למזוג לכבודו כוס
מיוחד כוס ישועה של הגאולה העתידה–הכל כדי לפרסם
בפני בני ביתו ולהודיעם שהגאולה שלמה תלויה בביאת
אליהו הנביא מקודם לבשר הגאולה והתגלות אליהו הנביא
תהיה האות על ביאת הגואל צדק.

Rabbi Yehudah Loew (Maharal of Prague), 1525–1609

Talmudist and philosopher. Maharal rose to prominence as leader of the
famed Jewish community of Prague. He is the author of more than a dozen
works of original philosophic thought, including *Tiferet Yisrael* and *Netsach
Yisrael.* He also authored *Gur Aryeh,* a supercommentary to Rashi's biblical
commentary; and a commentary on the nonlegal passages of the Talmud.
He is buried in the Old Jewish Cemetery of Prague.

I suggest the following explanation for this custom: The
Hallel *and* Nirtsah *sections of the* seder *are to arouse G-d's*
mercy and evoke our merit before G-d so that He redeem
us with the Final Redemption. For this reason, we must
let our children know and publicize our tradition from the
prophets that, prior to Mashiach's arrival, Elijah will come
and announce the Redemption. . . .

Scripture makes it clear that prior to Mashiach's arrival to
his "holy chamber," Elijah will arrive, and thus, his arrival
is the clear sign that Mashiach [who comes after] is the true
redeemer. . . . This is a fundamental piece in our messianic
belief and anticipation that guards us from falling into the
trap of a false messiah. Thus, the custom here is to open
the door for Elijah the Prophet and to pour a glass in his
honor, a special cup of redemption. The intent of it all is to
publicize to our families and let them know that the Final
Redemption is hinged upon Elijah coming to announce it.
Indeed, his arrival is the litmus test to gauge the legitimacy of
the righteous redeemer.

Elijah and the Redemption

TEXT 6

Malachi 3:23

הִנֵּה אָנֹכִי שֹׁלֵחַ לָכֶם אֵת אֵלִיָּה הַנָּבִיא לִפְנֵי בּוֹא יוֹם ה' הַגָּדוֹל וְהַנּוֹרָא:

Behold I will send you Elijah the Prophet before the coming of the great and awesome day of G-d.

Talmud, Tractate Eiruvin 43a–b

תא שמע הריני נזיר ביום שבן דוד בא מותר לשתות יין
בשבתות ובימים טובים, ואסור לשתות יין כל ימות החול.

אי אמרת בשלמא יש תחומין היינו דבשבתות ובימים
טובים מותר אלא אי אמרת אין תחומין בשבתות ובימים
טובים אמאי מותר?

שאני התם דאמר קרא הנה אנכי שלח לכם את אליה הנביא
וגו' והא לא אתא אליהו מאתמול.

אי הכי בחול כל יומא ויומא נמי לישתרי דהא לא אתא
אליהו מאתמול אלא אמרינן לבית דין הגדול אתא הכא נמי
לימא לבית דין הגדול אתא.

Come *and* **hear** *that which was taught in a Baraita: With regard to one who said,* **"I will be a Nazirite on the day that the son of David comes,"** *i.e., upon the arrival of the Messiah,* **he is permitted to drink wine on Shabbat and festivals,** *for the Messiah will not arrive on one of those days.*

Babylonian Talmud

A literary work of monumental proportions that draws upon the legal, spiritual, intellectual, ethical, and historical traditions of Judaism. The 37 tractates of the Babylonian Talmud contain the teachings of the Jewish sages from the period after the destruction of the 2nd Temple through the 5th century CE. It has served as the primary vehicle for the transmission of the Oral Law and the education of Jews over the centuries; it is the entry point for all subsequent legal, ethical, and theological Jewish scholarship.

However, he is prohibited to drink wine on all weekdays, *in case the Messiah has come and he has not yet been informed.*

The Talmud clarifies: Granted, if you say that *the prohibition of Shabbat* limits applies *above ten handbreadths,* that is *why* on Shabbat and festivals he is permitted *to drink wine, for the Messiah will certainly not arrive from outside the Shabbat limit on those days.* But if you say that *the prohibition of Shabbat* limits does not apply *above ten handbreadths,* why is he permitted *to drink wine* on Shabbat and festivals?

The Talmud answers: It is different there, as the verse stated, "Behold, I will send you Elijah the Prophet . . . *This verse teaches that Elijah will arrive the day before the coming of the Messiah.* Since Elijah did not come the previous day, *the Messiah will not come today, and therefore he may drink.*

The Talmud rejects this argument: If so, on weekdays, too, he should be permitted *to drink wine* each and every day, as Elijah did not arrive the previous day. Rather, *the reason for the prohibition on weekdays must be that* we say *that Elijah may already have* arrived at the Great Court, *but it has not yet become a matter of public knowledge.* Likewise, here too we should say *that Elijah already* arrived *the previous day* at the Great Court, *on the eve of Shabbat or a festival.*

TEXT 8

Rabbi Yonatan Eybeschutz, Kereti Upeleti,
Kuntres Bet Hasafek, *Conclusion*

ידוע מה שאמרו חז"ל "לא זכו בעתה, זכו אחישנה"... ודאי
סדר ותנאי ביאת משיח הוא שאליהו יבא לבשר ביאתו,
רק הני מילי אם נעשה בעתה, אבל אם זכו שימהר ויחיש
גאולה, מדלג על ההרים מקפץ על הגבעות לשנות הסדר,
ואהבה של קודשא בריך הוא כי זכו ישראל משנה השורה...
כי ודאי ראוי שאליהו יבא קודם לבשר, אבל אין מוחלט,
כי אולי ירחם ה להערות על ישראל רוח קדשו לעבדו בכל
לבב, ואז יחיש הפדות והגאולה, למהר ביאת בן דוד מבלי
בשורת אליהו ז"ל.

*Our sages' postulation that "If they are worthy, 'I will hasten
it'; if not, 'in its time'" is well known. . . . Now, Elijah's role to
announce the Redemption is certainly an integral part of the
messianic process, but it is only necessary if the Redemption
happens "in its time." However, if the Jews are worthy enough
to hasten the Redemption, G-d will "skip over mountains and
jump over hills" and change protocol, for the love G-d displays*

Rabbi Yonatan Eybeschutz, 1690–1764

Talmudist, authority on Jewish law, and kabbalist. Recognized during his
youth as a prodigy in Talmud, Rabbi Eybeschutz was appointed rabbinical
magistrate of Prague, and later rabbi of Metz. In 1750, he was elected rabbi
of Altona, Hamburg, and Wandsbek. He was surrounded by controversy
after Rabbi Yaakov Emden accused him of Sabbatean sympathies. Thirty
of his works were published, including *Urim Vetumim, Kereti Upeleti, Sar
Ha'alef* on the *Code of Jewish Law,* and *Ye'arot Devash,* a collection of his
sermons.

to His worthy people will bend the rules. . . . Of course, it is very much appropriate that Elijah arrive and announce the Redemption, but it is not necessary per se, for perhaps G-d will have mercy on His people and bestow upon them a holy spirit to rouse them to serve Him wholeheartedly. Then, the Redemption will be hastened, so that Mashiach can arrive even without Elijah's announcement.

Bridging Elijah from the Past

TEXT 9

Rabbi Baruch Epstein, Torah Temimah, *Numbers 25:12*

ויש לומר למאן דאמר פינחס זה אליהו ברכו בברכת השלום על פי מה שכתוב... אין אליהו בא אלא לעשות שלום בעולם. וזה ברכו כאן בסגולה זאת שיעשה שלום בעולם, והוא כתשלום גמול על השלום שעשה כביכול בין הקדוש ברוך הוא ובין ישראל ועצר המגפה.

Rabbi Baruch Epstein, 1860–1941

Son of Rabbi Yechiel Michel, author of the *Aruch Hashulchan*, Rabbi Epstein grew up in Novardok where his father served as rabbi. A bookkeeper by profession, he was an erudite scholar who authored a number of works, the most popular of which is his *Torah Temimah*, a *Chumash* that cites all Talmudic references to each verse, along with a running commentary.

According to the idea that Pinchas is the same person as Elijah, this "blessing of peace" is understood—based on the Talmud which states that Elijah will bring peace to the world. G-d blessed Pinchas with the privilege of restoring peace in the world in the future when Mashiach comes as a reward for the peace he restored between G-d and the Jewish people when he stopped the plague.

TEXT 10

The Rebbe, Rabbi Menachem Mendel Schneerson, Likutei Sichot 2, pp. 598–599

וואָס דאָס איז אויך אין דעם געדאַנק פון פנחס זה אליהו:

פנחס וואָס ענינו איז בריתי שלום, שלום ואחדות פון אין אידן מיטן צווייטן–זה אליהו, דאָס וועט ברענגען בקרוב ממש דעם מבשר אליהו הנביא וולכער וועט קומען אונז אָנזאָגן אז מאָרגן קומט משיח, אויסלייזן אונז בגאולה השלימה.

Rabbi Menachem Mendel Schneerson, 1902–1994

The towering Jewish leader of the 20th century, known as "the Lubavitcher Rebbe," or simply as "the Rebbe." Born in southern Ukraine, the Rebbe escaped Nazi-occupied Europe, arriving in the U.S. in June 1941. The Rebbe inspired and guided the revival of traditional Judaism after the European devastation, impacting virtually every Jewish community the world over. The Rebbe often emphasized that the performance of just one additional good deed could usher in the era of Mashiach. The Rebbe's scholarly talks and writings have been printed in more than 200 volumes.

This is the significance of the idea that "Pinchas is Elijah":

Pinchas was a man of peace, namely peace and harmony between one Jew and another. This harmony "is Elijah"; namely, it will bring Elijah, the one who will come and tell us that Mashiach is coming tomorrow and taking us out of exile, may it be very soon!

4

ELIJAH THE
PROPHET PART II

Harbinger of the Redemption

A Man of Many Roles

TEXT 1

Mishnah, Tractate Eduyot 8:7

אָמַר רַבִּי יְהוֹשֻׁעַ, מְקֻבָּל אֲנִי מֵרַבָּן יוֹחָנָן בֶּן זַכַּאי, שֶׁשָּׁמַע מֵרַבּוֹ וְרַבּוֹ מֵרַבּוֹ, הֲלָכָה לְמשֶׁה מִסִּינַי, שֶׁאֵין אֵלִיָּהוּ בָא לְטַמֵּא וּלְטַהֵר, לְרַחֵק וּלְקָרֵב, אֶלָּא לְרַחֵק הַמְקֹרָבִין בִּזְרוֹעַ וּלְקָרֵב הַמְרֻחָקִין בִּזְרוֹעַ. מִשְׁפַּחַת בֵּית צְרִיפָה הָיְתָה בְעֵבֶר הַיַּרְדֵּן וְרִחֲקָהּ בֶּן צִיּוֹן בִּזְרוֹעַ, וְעוֹד אַחֶרֶת הָיְתָה שָׁם וְקֵרְבָהּ בֶּן צִיּוֹן בִּזְרוֹעַ. כְּגוֹן אֵלּוּ, אֵלִיָּהוּ בָא לְטַמֵּא וּלְטַהֵר, לְרַחֵק וּלְקָרֵב.

Mishnah

The first authoritative work of Jewish law that was codified in writing. The Mishnah contains the oral traditions that were passed down from teacher to student; it supplements, clarifies, and systematizes the commandments of the Torah. Due to the continual persecution of the Jewish people, it became increasingly difficult to guarantee that these traditions would not be forgotten. Rabbi Yehudah Hanassi therefore redacted the Mishnah at the end of the 2nd century. It serves as the foundation for the Talmud.

רַבִּי יְהוּדָה אוֹמֵר, לְקָרֵב, אֲבָל לֹא לְרַחֵק.

רַבִּי שִׁמְעוֹן אוֹמֵר, לְהַשְׁווֹת הַמַּחֲלֶקֶת.

וַחֲכָמִים אוֹמְרִים, לֹא לְרַחֵק וְלֹא לְקָרֵב, אֶלָּא לַעֲשׂוֹת שָׁלוֹם
בָּעוֹלָם, שֶׁנֶּאֱמַר "הִנֵּה אָנֹכִי שֹׁלֵחַ לָכֶם אֶת אֵלִיָּה הַנָּבִיא וְגוֹ'
וְהֵשִׁיב לֵב אָבוֹת עַל בָּנִים וְלֵב בָּנִים עַל אֲבוֹתָם".

Rabbi Joshua said, "I have received a tradition from Rabban
Yochanan ben Zakkai, who heard it from his teacher, and
his teacher [heard it] from his teacher, as a halachah [given]
to Moses from Sinai, that Elijah will not come to pronounce
unclean or to pronounce clean, to put away or to bring near,
but to put away those brought near by force and to bring
near those put away by force. The family of Beth Tsriphah
was on the other side of the Jordan, and Ben Zion put it away
by force; and yet another family was there, and Ben Zion
brought it near by force. It is [cases] such as these that Elijah
will come to pronounce unclean or to pronounce clean, to
put away or to bring near."

Rabbi Judah says, "To bring near, but not to put away."

Rabbi Shimon says, "To conciliate disputes."

And the sages say, "Neither to put away nor to bring near,
but to make peace in the world, for it is said, 'Behold, I send
to you Elijah the Prophet,' etc., 'and he shall turn the heart
of the fathers to the children and the heart of the children to
their fathers.'"

TEXT 2

Maimonides, Commentary to Eduyot ad loc.

וחכמים אומרים אין עושק ביוחסין כל הנקרא בשמו הכל
יתיחסו אל האמת והתורה שהיא אב הכל אבל ההתעשקות
והרעות הם השנאות שבין בני אדם לפי שהם חנם והוא
חומס בשנאתו אותו והוא אמרם לעשות שלום בעולם.

The sages say that there are no injustices with regard to lineage; rather, everyone's assumed lineage will ultimately be traced to the truth, for the Torah is the parent of all truth. Rather, the injustices Elijah will indeed arbitrate will be wrongdoings between one person and another, for they are petty, causing one to destroy another with their hatred. Elijah will come to remove this hatred and restore peace.

Rabbi Moshe ben Maimon, (Maimonides, Rambam), 1135–1204

Halachist, philosopher, author, and physician. Maimonides was born in Córdoba, Spain. After the conquest of Córdoba by the Almohads, he fled Spain and eventually settled in Cairo, Egypt. There, he became the leader of the Jewish community and served as court physician to the vizier of Egypt. He is most noted for authoring the *Mishneh Torah,* an encyclopedic arrangement of Jewish law; and for his philosophical work, *Guide for the Perplexed.* His rulings on Jewish law are integral to the formation of halachic consensus.

TEXT 3

Jerusalem Talmud, Tractate Shabbat 9a

תחיית המתים לידי אליהו ז"ל. דכתיב "הנה אנכי שולח
לכם את אליה הנביא לפני בוא יום ה' הגדול והנורא והשיב
לב אבות על בנים ולב בנים על אבותם".

*Resurrection of the dead brings us to Elijah, as it is stated,
"Lo, I will send you Elijah the Prophet before the coming of
the great and awesome day of G-d. That he may turn the
heart of the fathers back through the children, and the heart
of the children back through their fathers."*

Jerusalem Talmud

A commentary to the Mishnah, compiled during the 4th and 5th centuries.
The Jerusalem Talmud predates its Babylonian counterpart by 100 years
and is written in both Hebrew and Aramaic. While the Babylonian Talmud is
the most authoritative source for Jewish law, the Jerusalem Talmud remains
an invaluable source for the spiritual, intellectual, ethical, historical, and legal
traditions of Judaism.

Rabbi Yom Tov Lippman Heller, Tosafot
Yom Tov *to Eduyot, ad loc.*

שלא תהיה עוד מחלוקת ביניהם. [ונראה לי דמהכא רגילין
לומר דתיק"ו שאמרו בגמרא היא נוטריקון תשבי יתרץ
קושיות ואבעיות אף על פי שמשמעותה נ"ל תהא קאי.
כנוטריקון דדייתיקי. שפירש הר"ב במשנה ז' בפ"ק דב"מ.
וכלומר שהקושיא קאי ובמקומה עומדת].

*Elijah will end all disagreement. This is the basis for the pop-
ular notion that the word* "תיקו" *mentioned in the Talmud is
an acronym for* "תשבי יתרץ קושיות ואבעיות"—*The Tishbite will
resolve all questions and inquiries." The simple interpretation
reads it as a portmanteau of the words* "תהא קאי"—*leave the
matter at status quo."*

Rabbi Yom Tov Lippman Heller, 1579–1654

Authority on Jewish law, author, flourished in Poland and Germany, often
called the *Tosafot Yom Tov* after the title of this most famous work on the
Mishnah. In his youth, he was a student of the Maharal of Prague. In addition
to his profound mastery of the Talmud and post-Talmudic commentaries, he
was engaged in the study of kabbalah, philosophy, and grammar and had a
broad grasp of mathematics, astronomy, and natural science. At 18, he was
appointed rabbinic judge in Prague and served there for almost 28 years.
Later, he served as rabbi in Nikolsburg, Vienna, Lublin, Brisk, Ludmir, and
other communities.

TEXT 5

Zohar, Raya Mehemna 3, p. 28a

ואליהו הוא יהיה לי לפה, ייתי לתקנא כל אלין ספיקות
ולפרקא לון בההוא זמנא.

Elijah will be Moses's mouthpiece; namely, at that time, he will come and resolve all unsolved questions.

Zohar

The seminal work of kabbalah, Jewish mysticism. The *Zohar* is a mystical commentary on the Torah, written in Aramaic and Hebrew. According to the Arizal, the *Zohar* contains the teachings of Rabbi Shimon bar Yocha'i, who lived in the Land of Israel during the 2nd century. The *Zohar* has become one of the indispensable texts of traditional Judaism, alongside and nearly equal in stature to the Mishnah and Talmud.

When Will
He Come?

TEXT 6

Maimonides, Mishneh Torah, *Laws
of Kings and Wars 12:2*

יראה מפשוטן של דברי הנביאים שבתחילת ימות המשיח
תהיה מלחמת גוג ומגוג ושקודם מלחמת גוג ומגוג יעמוד
נביא לישר ישראל ולהכין לבם שנאמר הנה אנכי שולח
לכם את אליה וגו'...

ויש מן החכמים שאומרים שקודם ביאת המשיח יבא
אליהו וכל אלו הדברים וכיוצא בהן לא ידע אדם איך יהיו
עד שיהיו שדברים סתומין הן אצל הנביאים גם החכמים
אין להם קבלה בדברים אלו אלא לפי הכרע הפסוקים
ולפיכך יש להם מחלוקת בדברים אלו ועל כל פנים אין
סדור הויית דברים אלו ולא דקדוקיהן עיקר בדת ולעולם
לא יתעסק אדם בדברי ההגדות ולא יאריך במדרשות
האמורים בענינים אלו וכיוצא בהן ולא ישימם עיקר שאין
מביאין לא לידי יראה ולא לידי אהבה.

The simple interpretation of the prophet's words appears to imply that the war of Gog and Magog will take place at the beginning of the messianic age [after Mashiach's arrival]. Before the war of Gog and Magog, a prophet will arise to inspire Israel to be upright and prepare their hearts, as Scripture states, "Behold, I am sending you Elijah." . . .

[By contrast,] there are some sages who say that Elijah's coming will precede Mashiach's arrival.

All these and similar matters cannot be definitely known by man until they occur, for these matters are undefined in the prophet's words, and even the wise men have no established tradition regarding these matters except their own interpretation of the verses. Therefore, there is a controversy among them regarding these matters.

Regardless of the debate concerning these questions, neither the order of the occurrence of these events nor their precise detail are among the fundamental principles of the faith. A person should not occupy himself with the Agadot and homiletics concerning these and similar matters, nor should he consider them as essentials, for study of them will neither bring fear nor love of G-d.

Why Elijah?

TEXT 7

The Rebbe, Rabbi Menachem Mendel Schneerson,
Torat Menachem 34 (5722:3), p. 114

שייכותו של אליהו הנביא לבשורת הגאולה מובנת גם על
פי מה שנתבאר לעיל החילוק בין משה ואליהו שמשה רבינו
אף על פי שכשנולד נתמלא הבית כולו אור, הרי זה לא חדר
בהגשמי עצמו, שלכן היה גופו טעון קבורה. מה שאין כן
אליהו בחינת ובגימטריא ב"ן שפעל הזיכוך בגופו הגשמי

Rabbi Menachem Mendel Schneerson, 1902–1994

The towering Jewish leader of the 20th century, known as "the Lubavitcher Rebbe," or simply as "the Rebbe." Born in southern Ukraine, the Rebbe escaped Nazi-occupied Europe, arriving in the U.S. in June 1941. The Rebbe inspired and guided the revival of traditional Judaism after the European devastation, impacting virtually every Jewish community the world over. The Rebbe often emphasized that the performance of just one additional good deed could usher in the era of Mashiach. The Rebbe's scholarly talks and writings have been printed in more than 200 volumes.

ועד שעלה בסערה השמימה. וזהו הקשר לגאולה העתידה,
שענינה הוא "וראו כל בשר", שהבשר הגשמי יזדכך כל כך
עד שיראה אלקות.

Elijah's unique association with heralding the Redemption can be understood by way of explaining the difference between him and Moses: When Moses was born, the house was filled with light, but at the end of the day, that light didn't penetrate his material body, and thus, his body was ultimately buried.

Elijah, by contrast, was of different cloth; he transformed his material body, so much so, that he ascended alive to the Heavens.

This, then, is his connection to the Redemption, for the Redemption is all about "All flesh together shall see [that the mouth of G-d spoke]," namely that the material flesh will be transformed so much that it will actually see G-dliness.

TEXT 8

The Rebbe, Rabbi Menachem Mendel
Schneerson, Likutei Sichot 30, *p. 172, fn 27*

מצינו כמה ענינים שבאים בתור הכנה לימות המשיח,
ובלשון הרמב"ם (בנוגע לאליהו) "ליישר ישראל ולהכין
לבם" לימות המשיח, וכל שכן וקל וחומר שכן צריך להיות
בנוגע לענינים העיקרי של ימות המשיח - "לא נתאוו
החכמים והנביאים ימות המשיח... אלא כדי שיהיו פנויין
בתורה וחכמתה" שיוכלו לעסוק בהשגת "דעת בוראם"
שצריכים "ליישר ישראל ולהכין לבם" לכך.

There are a number of items that we find as preparatory steps
for Mashiach. In Maimonides's words, Elijah's role will be "to
align the people and prepare their hearts" for the messianic
era. It certainly must be so regarding the primary matter of
the messianic era, namely, [what Maimonides describes as,]
"The sages yearned for the messianic era only so that . . .
they be free to engage in Torah wisdom," the opportunity to
engage in understanding "the knowledge of their Creator."
It is necessary to "align the Jewish people and prepare their
hearts" for that.

Midrash, Shochar Tov, *Psalm 43*

שלחת הגאולה [ביציאת מצרים] על ידי ב' גואלים שנאמר
"שלח משה עבדו אהרן אשר בחר בו", גם לדור הזה
שלח שנים...

וכן הוא אומר "הנה אנכי שולח לכם את אליהו הנביא וגו'",
הרי אחד, והשני "הן עבדי אתמך בו", לכך נאמר "שלח
אורך ואמתך וגו'".

The original redemption [from Egypt] was effected by two redeemers, as the verse states, "He sent Moses His servant [and] Aaron whom He chose." So it will be in this generation, two redeemers will be sent.

Indeed, the verse states, "I will send Elijah the Prophet to you . . ."—that's one. The second, "Behold My servant, I will support him." It is for this reason that the verse states, "Send your light and your truth."

Shochar Tov, (Midrash Tehillim)

An agadic Midrash on Psalms, containing homilies on verses and individual words. It is an old work, known since the 11th century when it was cited by Rashi and other scholars.

TEXT 10

Rabbi Menachem Nachum Twersky of Chernobyl, Me'or *Einayim,* Pinchas

הנה אנכי שולח לכם את אליהו הנביא לפני בא וגו' דלשון
שולח כתיב לשון הווה דמשמע אף עכשיו מדלא כתיב
אשלח לכם וגו' דהאמת הוא שכל השתוקקות ישראל
עובדי ה' לאביהם שבשמים הוא על ידי בחינת אליהו שהוא
המבשר לכל דבר שהוא שלימות כגון תורה ותפלה...
ומקודם זה צריך תשוקה גדולה וחשק גדול, וזה הוא על
ידי בחינת אליהו המעורר התשוקה מקודם, ואחר כך הוא
בחינת משיח... כמאמר הבעש"ט נבג"מ שצריך כל אחד
מישראל לתקן ולהכין חלק קומת משיח השייך לנשמתו...
יהיה משיח קומה שלימה מכל נשמות ישראל כלולה מס'
ריבוא... על כן צריך כל אחד מישראל להכין חלק בחינת
משיח השייך לחלק נשמתו עד שיתוקן ותכונן כל הקומה
ויהיה יחוד כללי בתמידות במהרה בימינו...

וזה אי אפשר אם לא על ידי התשוקה שמקודם שהוא
בחינת המבשר בחינת אליהו... ולכך קודם השלימות
הגמור יהיה בשורת אליהו ז"ל להתעורר תשוקת ישראל
קודם ביאת משיח.

Rabbi Menachem Nachum Twersky of Chernobyl, 1730–1797

Born in Garinsk, Ukraine; Chasidic rebbe, founder of the Chernobyl dynasty;
student of the Baal Shem Tov and of the Magid of Mezeritch. Orphaned
as a child, he was raised by his uncle Nachum, who educated him in the
style of the great Lithuanian *yeshivot*. His book, *Me'or Einayim*, comprised
of insights on the weekly Torah portion, is a Chasidic classic. He was
succeeded by his son, Rabbi Mordechai Twersky.

[The verse states,] "Lo, I will send you Elijah the Prophet before the coming. . . ." The word "שולח—I will send" as opposed to "אשלח" is actually written in the present tense, which implies that it's already happening now. The truth is that all inspiration any Jew has toward their Father in Heaven is the element of Elijah "announcing" all matters of perfection, like Torah and prayer. . . . Prior to perfection, there must be much yearning and desire—and that comes through Elijah, who inspires this great drive. Only after that does the element of Mashiach arrive. . . . As the Baal Shem Tov stated, "Every Jew ought to prepare and polish the portion of Mashiach that is directly related to their soul." . . . Mashiach's actual arrival is the culmination of the individual souls of all 600,000 Jews. . . . For this reason, every Jew must work with the portion of Mashiach that is relevant to their soul until the entire collective body is unified constantly, may it be soon in our days. . . .

Such unity is impossible without a great amount of prior inspiration. This inspiration is called an "announcement," and it is Elijah's role. . . . Thus, prior to the perfection of Mashiach, Elijah's announcement will come to inspire the Jews' great yearning and desire.

5

THE GRAND BANQUET

Unpacking the Feast
of the Future

The Basics

TEXT 1

Midrash, Vayikra Rabah *13:3*

אָמַר רַבִּי יוּדָן בְּרַבִּי שִׁמְעוֹן כָּל בְּהֵמוֹת וְלִוְיָתָן הֵן קְנִיגִין שֶׁל צַדִּיקִים לֶעָתִיד לָבוֹא... כֵּיצַד הֵם נִשְׁחָטִים, בְּהֵמוֹת נוֹתֵץ לַלִּוְיָתָן בְּקַרְנָיו וְקוֹרְעוֹ, וְלִוְיָתָן נוֹתֵץ לַבְּהֵמוֹת בִּסְנַפִּירָיו וְנוֹחֲרוֹ.

וַחֲכָמִים אוֹמְרִים זוֹ שְׁחִיטָה כְּשֵׁרָה הִיא, וְלֹא כָּךְ תָּנִינַן הַכֹּל שׁוֹחֲטִין וּבַכֹּל שׁוֹחֲטִין וּלְעוֹלָם שׁוֹחֲטִין חוּץ מִמַּגַּל קָצִיר, וְהַמְּגֵרָה, וְהַשִּׁנַּיִם, מִפְּנֵי שֶׁהֵן חוֹנְקִין. אָמַר רַבִּי אָבִין בַּר כַּהֲנָא אָמַר הַקָּדוֹשׁ בָּרוּךְ הוּא: תּוֹרָה חֲדָשָׁה מֵאִתִּי תֵצֵא, חִדּוּשׁ תּוֹרָה מֵאִתִּי תֵצֵא.

Vayikra Rabah

An early rabbinic commentary on the Book of Leviticus. This Midrash, written in Aramaic and Hebrew, provides textual exegeses and anecdotes, expounds upon the biblical narrative, and develops and illustrates moral principles. It was first printed in Constantinople in 1512 together with 4 other Midrashic works on the other 4 books of the Pentateuch.

Rabbi Yudan said in the name of Rabbi Shimon, "The behe-moth *and the leviathan will be game for the righteous in the World to Come. . . .*

"How are they slaughtered? The behemoth *gores the levia-than with its horns and shreds it, and the leviathan impales the* behemoth *with its fins and slaughters it."*

The sages asked, "Is this a kosher slaughtering? The Mishnah states, 'All may slaughter; and with any implement one may slaughter, except a scythe, a saw, teeth, or a fingernail, since these strangle.'"

Rabbi Avin said in the name of Bar Kahana, "G-d says, 'For new teachings shall go forth from Me; novel parts of Torah will go forth from Me.'"

TEXT 2

Talmud, Tractate Pesachim 119b

עתיד הקדוש ברוך הוא לעשות סעודה לצדיקים ביום
שיגמל חסדו לזרעו של יצחק.

Babylonian Talmud

A literary work of monumental proportions that draws upon the legal, spiritual, intellectual, ethical, and historical traditions of Judaism. The 37 tractates of the Babylonian Talmud contain the teachings of the Jewish sages from the period after the destruction of the 2nd Temple through the 5th century CE. It has served as the primary vehicle for the transmission of the Oral Law and the education of Jews over the centuries; it is the entry point for all subsequent legal, ethical, and theological Jewish scholarship.

לאחר שאוכלין ושותין, נותנין לו לאברהם אבינו כוס של
ברכה לברך ואומר להן איני מברך שיצא ממני ישמעאל.

אומר לו ליצחק טול וברך. אומר להן איני מברך
שיצא ממני עשו.

אומר לו ליעקב טול וברך. אומר להם איני מברך שנשאתי
שתי אחיות בחייהן שעתידה תורה לאוסרן עלי.

אומר לו למשה טול וברך. אומר להם איני מברך שלא זכיתי
ליכנס לארץ ישראל לא בחיי ולא במותי.

אומר לו ליהושע טול וברך. אומר להן איני מברך שלא
זכיתי לבן...

אומר לו לדוד טול וברך. אומר להן אני אברך ולי נאה לברך
שנאמר "כוס ישועות אשא ובשם ה' אקרא".

*In the future, G-d will prepare a feast for the righteous on the
day that He extends His mercy to the descendants of Isaac.*

*After they eat and drink, the celebrants will give Abraham
our father a cup of blessing to recite the blessing. Abraham
will say to them, "I will not recite the blessing, for the wicked
Ishmael came from me."*

*Abraham will say to Isaac, "Take the cup and recite the
blessing." Isaac will say to them, "I will not recite the blessing,
as the wicked Esau came from me."*

*Isaac will say to Jacob, "Take the cup and recite the blessing."
Jacob will say to them, "I will not recite the blessing, as I*

married two sisters in their lifetimes, and the Torah would later forbid them to me."

Jacob will say to Moses, "Take the cup and recite the blessing." Moses will say to them, "I will not recite the blessing, as I did not merit to enter Israel, neither in my life nor in my death."

Moses will say to Joshua, "Take the cup and recite the blessing." Joshua will say to them, "I will not recite the blessing, as I did not merit to have a son. . . ."

Joshua will say to David, "Take the cup and recite the blessing." David will say to them, "I will recite the blessing, and it is fitting for me to recite the blessing, as it is stated, 'I will lift up the cup of salvation, and I will call upon the name of G-d.'"

TEXT 3

Maimonides, Mishneh Torah,
Laws of Repentance 8:3–4

הטובה, שאין אחריה טובה, והיא שהתאוו לה כל הנביאים...
[ו]חכמים קראו לה דרך משל... סעודה.

Rabbi Moshe ben Maimon (Maimonides, Rambam), 1135–1204

Halachist, philosopher, author, and physician. Maimonides was born in Córdoba, Spain. After the conquest of Córdoba by the Almohads, he fled Spain and eventually settled in Cairo, Egypt. There, he became the leader of the Jewish community and served as court physician to the vizier of Egypt. He is most noted for authoring the *Mishneh Torah,* an encyclopedic arrangement of Jewish law; and for his philosophical work, *Guide for the Perplexed.* His rulings on Jewish law are integral to the formation of halachic consensus.

The good beyond which there can be [other] good. This was [the good] desired by all the prophets. . . . The sages referred to this good, which is prepared for the righteous, by the metaphor "feast."

TEXT 4

Rabbi Shmuel Eliezer Halevi Eidels,
Chidushei Agadot to Bava Batra 44b

דע כי יש לנו להאמין בכל הדברים האלו בפשטן ואף
שהמפרשים האריכו בדרוש הזה לפי כוונתם יעוין שם אין
הדברים יוצאין ממשמען.

Know this: We ought to believe all these matters in their simple literal sense. Though many commentaries interpret it in various ways, they do not supplant the plain meaning.

Rabbi Shmuel Eliezer Halevi Eidels (Maharsha), 1555–1632

Rabbi, author, and Talmudist. Rabbi Eidels established a yeshiva in Posen, Poland, which was supported by his mother-in-law, Eidel (hence his surname is "Eidel's"). He is primarily known for his *Chidushei Halachot,* a commentary on the Talmud in which he resolves difficulties in the texts of the Talmud, Rashi, and *Tosafot,* and which is a basic work for those who seek an in-depth understanding of the Talmud; and for his *Chidushei Agadot,* his innovative commentary on the homiletic passages of the Talmud.

A Giant Fish, Ox, and Extraordinary Wine

TEXT 5

Talmud, Tractate Bava Batra 74b

אמר רב יהודה אמר רב כל מה שברא הקדוש ברוך הוא
בעולמו זכר ונקבה בראם, אף לויתן נחש בריח ולויתן נחש
עקלתון זכר ונקבה בראם, ואלמלי נזקקין זה לזה מחריבין
כל העולם כולו. מה עשה הקדוש ברוך הוא? סירס את
הזכר והרג הנקבה ומלחה לצדיקים לעתיד לבא, שנאמר
"והרג את התנין אשר בים"...

Rav Yehudah said in the name of Rav, "Everything that the Holy One, blessed be He, created in His world, He created male and female. Even leviathan the rod serpent and leviathan the tortuous serpent He created male and female. Had they coupled and produced offspring, they would have destroyed the entire world. What did the Holy One, blessed be He, do? He castrated the male and killed the female, and salted the female to preserve it for the banquet for the righteous in the future. As it is stated, 'And He will slay the serpent that is in the sea.'"

TEXT 6

Talmud, Tractate Berachot 34b

מאי "עין לא ראתה"?

אמר רבי יהושע בן לוי: זה יין המשומר בענביו מששת ימי בראשית.

What is this reward about which it is stated, "No eye has seen it"?

Rabbi Yehoshua ben Levi said, "That is the wine that has been preserved in its grapes since the six days of Creation and which no eye has ever seen."

A Mystical Meal with Meaningful Messages

TEXT 7

Rabbi Yehudah Lowe, Netsach Yisrael, *ch. 33*

העולם הזה אין ראוי שיהיה העולם אחד, עד זמן המלך
המשיח, ואז "לא ישא גוי אל גוי חרב", ויהיה העולם אחד,
בלא שום חלוק ופירוד...

אבל הענין הזה... וסעודה זאת, רוצה לומר השכר על
מה שהגיע להם מן הצרה בגלותם, וקבלת שכר על זה,

Rabbi Yehudah Lowe (Maharal of Prague), 1525–1609

Talmudist and philosopher. Maharal rose to prominence as leader of the famed Jewish community of Prague. He is the author of more than a dozen works of original philosophic thought, including *Tiferet Yisrael* and *Netsach Yisrael*. He also authored *Gur Aryeh,* a supercommentary to Rashi's biblical commentary; and a commentary on the nonlegal passages of the Talmud. He is buried in the Old Jewish Cemetery of Prague.

שאוכלים את שכרם [מחמת] שהיו בצרה - נקרא זה
'סעודה'. והסעודה הזאת אינה גשמית, רק קבול השכר
נקרא שעושה להם סעודה...

וזה שאמר אחרי שאכלו ושתו נותנים כוס לאברהם לברך.
כלומר כל סעודה יש ברכה... כי מפני הברכה שנתן השם
יתברך לאדם, יש לו לברך השם יתברך אשר מאתו הברכה...

ואין בכל הצדיקים כמו דוד. שכל הצדיקים היה להם חסרון
בדבר מה. ואין זה נחשב חסרון במעלתם, שכל כך היה להם
מעלה עליונה, עד שאותה מעלה אי אפשר שתהיה בלא
חסרון, וכמו שיתבאר. אבל לדוד לא היה חסרון, ולכך ראוי
לברך אל הממציא מאתו הברכה... כי כל ענין דוד היה מעין
דוגמא של מלך המשיח לעתיד... ולכן יצא ממנו המלך
המשיח, שיהיה משלים העולם שיהיה בלא חסרון. וזהו
עיקר מעלתו של עולם שיהיה לעתיד.

*This world is not meant to be a unified, perfect world until
Mashiach comes. Then, there will be no war; rather, it will be
a unified world without any division or fragmentation. . . .*

*[This, then, is the idea of the future banquet.] "Banquet"
means "reward" for enduring the tremendous suffering of
exile. Receiving this reward is called a "banquet." This banquet is not a physical thing, rather a time to receive reward,
which can be called "banquet." . . .*

*In line with this, the participants of this "banquet" offer a
cup to Abraham to recite Grace, for every meal is followed*

with blessing . . . for a person ought to thank G-d, the source of all blessing.

There were no other tsadikim *[righteous people] like David. All others possessed a certain deficiency. This doesn't detract from their greatness; to the contrary—they were so great that it was only inevitable that their greatness would entail some sort of deficiency. David, by contrast, had no deficiencies, and thus, he is best suited to recite Grace. . . . King David was similar to the future King Mashiach . . . which is why Mashiach will descend from him. David and Mashiach share the theme of bringing the world to perfection, which is the principal quality of future times.*

TEXT 8

Rabbi Levi Yitschak of Berditchev,
Kedushat Levi, Likutim

כי סעודות צדיקים לעתיד לבוא יהיה על שני בחינות, אחד,
על פי פשוט סעודות ממש, ואחד, שישיגו ישראל סודות
התורה והסעודות יהיה על רוחניות כמבואר בזוהר הקדוש.

Rabbi Levi Yitschak of Berditchev, 1740–1809

Chasidic rebbe. Rabbi Levi Yitschak was one of the foremost disciples of the Magid of Mezeritch and later went on to serve as rabbi in Berditchev, Ukraine. His Chasidic commentary on the Torah, *Kedushat Levi,* is a classic that is popular to this day. He is known in Jewish history and folklore for his all-encompassing love, compassion, and advocacy on behalf of the Jewish people.

והנה שניהם אמת, האנשים אשר הם במדריגה קטנה
שהתענוג שלהם מגשמיות להם יהיה הסעודה סעודה
ממש, והצדיקים הגדולים אשר תענוג שלהם סודות התורה
להם יהיה הסעודה כאשר ישיגו נפלאות מתורתו הקדושה.

The future banquet for the righteous will be experienced on two levels: one, as a simple meal, and another, it will be a spiritual opportunity to uncover the secrets of Torah (as explained in the Zohar).

They are both true: For more ordinary folk, whose conception of pleasure is limited to the material, it will be a physical meal. For the righteous, whose conception of pleasure is secrets of Torah, the "meal" will be an opportunity to uncover great wonders of the Torah.

Rabbi Shne'ur Zalman of Liadi,
Likutei Torah *18a–b*

כי יש ב' מיני צדיקים הא' אותן שהם בסתר שעבודתם
ברוחניות פירוש בכוונת הלב לייחד יחודים עליונים
ובבחינת עליות וכגון רשב"י כשהיה במערה י"ג שנה
שבודאי לא היה יכול לקיים במעשה כמה מצות מעשיות
שהרי לא היו ניזונים רק מחרובא ועינא דמיא דאיברי להן
אם כן לא קיים אכילת מצה בפסח וקדוש על היין ואתרוג
וסוכה כו'...

והב' הם אותן צדיקים שהן בגילוי שעבודתם בגשמיות
בקיום המצות מעשיות... שהוא גם כן המשכת
אורות עליונים..

הנה הילוך הצדיקים הנקראים נוני ימא היא נפלאה וגבוה
מאד, כמו על דרך משל הדגים ששטים בים כך הם
שטים ובטיסה אחת מגיע למעלה מעלה וגדולה הרבה
מעבודת הצדיקים שבגשמיות שמחה בבשר כו' שהכל
למטה במדרגה...

Rabbi Shne'ur Zalman of Liadi (Alter Rebbe), 1745–1812

Chasidic rebbe, halachic authority, and founder of the Chabad movement.
The Alter Rebbe was born in Liozna, Belarus, and was among the principal
students of the Magid of Mezeritch. His numerous works include the *Tanya,*
an early classic containing the fundamentals of Chabad Chasidism; and
Shulchan Aruch HaRav, an expanded and reworked code of Jewish law.

ולעתיד הלויתן יעשה מלחמה עם שור הבר וישחטנו
בסנפיריו, כי הנה עבודת הצדיקים שבבחי' השנית נק' שור
הבר... כי הנה גם עבודתם במעשה גשמיות... אינו כפשוטו
שיאכל בשר השור למלאות בטנו ח"ו וישיש בו, אלא
בחינת העלאות... דהיינו שמחה לה' הנולד מזה ברשפי אש
והתלהבות כו'... ולכן הלויתן ישחוט את שור הבר, פירוש
שיעלה אותו...

אך באמת גם שור הבר יעלה את הלויתן כי בבחינה אחת
עבודתם נעלית יותר אף שהיא בבחינת עבודה גשמיית,
הרי כן צריך להיות על פי התורה ושמחת בחגך ואין שמחה
אלא בבשר ויין כו', ומצד זה יעלה הוא אותו.

There are two types of tsadikim: *The hidden ones, whose
religious service is spiritual in nature, namely with the intent
of spiritual unifications. Rabbi Shimon bar Yocha'i who hid
in a cave for thirteen years was one such* tsadik. *While there,
he certainly couldn't fulfill any* mitzvot; *after all, he lived
off a carob tree and a stream created especially for him. He
couldn't eat matzah on Passover, make Kiddush on wine,
nor shake a lulav and etrog on Sukkot. . . .*

The second type of tsadik *are those in plain view; they engage
with material matter, performing physical* mitzvot . . . *which
also draws down intense G-dly energy. . . .*

Now, the former type of tsadik, *called "creature of the sea,"
climbs to dizzying heights. Like fish that swiftly swim from
one end of the sea to the other, these* tsadikim *swiftly climb*

to greater heights than those who work with the material, bogged down as they are with lowly matter. . . .

In future times, the leviathan will battle the shor habar *and slaughter it with his fins: The second type of* tsadik *is represented by the* shor habar . . . *whose engagement with material matter . . . is obviously not simply to fill their bellies with meat and revel in it, G-d forbid, rather to sublimate it . . . namely to fuel a passionate rejoicing with G-d. . . . [Inasmuch as their path is inferior to the spiritual* tsadik,] *the leviathan will thus slaughter the* shor habar, *namely she will elevate it. . . .*

The reality is that the shor habar *will also elevate the leviathan, for in a certain way, the "shor habar tsadik" performs a greater service. Though his path is mired in material matter, the fact is that this is what the Torah prescribes, "You shall rejoice in your festivals—joy is only with meat and wine." From this perspective, the* shor habar *will elevate the leviathan.*

TEXT 10

The Rebbe, Rabbi Menachem Mendel Schneerson, Sefer Hasichot *5751:2, p. 582*

שחיטת שור הבר היא תוכן הסך-הכל דכללות מעשינו
ועבודתינו בבירור העולם, ולכן, יתגלה בזה תכלית
השלימות דכללות העבודה שגם העניינים הכי נעלים...
לויתן, עלמא דאתכסייא יומשכו באופן של... שור הבר,
עלמא דאתגלייא.

The leviathan slaughtering the shor habar *is the sum total of our entire work [during exile] of transforming the world. Then, the ultimate power of our religious devotion will be revealed, namely that the loftiest levels [of G-dliness] . . . like the leviathan of the hidden world, will be exposed in the manner . . . of the* shor habar—*in a revealed way.*

Rabbi Menachem Mendel Schneerson, 1902–1994

The towering Jewish leader of the 20th century, known as "the Lubavitcher Rebbe," or simply as "the Rebbe." Born in southern Ukraine, the Rebbe escaped Nazi-occupied Europe, arriving in the U.S. in June 1941. The Rebbe inspired and guided the revival of traditional Judaism after the European devastation, impacting virtually every Jewish community the world over. The Rebbe often emphasized that the performance of just one additional good deed could usher in the era of Mashiach. The Rebbe's scholarly talks and writings have been printed in more than 200 volumes.

Appendix: More Explanations for the Grand Banquet

Rabbi Shmuel Yissochor Dov Taubenfeld, 1930–1985

Born in Galicia, Rabbi Taubenfeld's family was exiled to Siberia, where
they spent the war years. Taubenfeld eventually made his way to Monsey,
N.Y., where he was a student of the renowned Talmudic scholar Rabbi
Reuven Grozovsky. Taubenfeld served as the leader of the Kehal Charedim
community in Monsey. Selections of his teachings were published
posthumously under the title *Zichron Shmuel*.

וענין שור הבר נראה לומר בדרך אפשר דהנה כתיב פני
השור מהשמאל, והרמז בזה כי שור מורה על מדת היראה
והפחד דהוא מסטרא דשמאלא, נמצא לפי זה דלויתן קאי
על אהבה ושור הבר על יראה.

וענין סעודת שור הבר ולויתן יחד היינו שיתכללו היראה
באהבה והאהבה ביראה, כי באמת יראה ואהבה הם תרתי
דסתרי אם יש יראה אין אהבה, ואם יש אהבה אין יראה,
אבל בעבודת ה' יכול להיות שניהם ביחד, יראה ואהבה ואין
ביניהם סתירה.

Rabbeinu Bechaye speaks about the feast of the leviathan, explaining the significance of the leviathan. He writes that the meaning can be found in the translation of the word which means "connection," namely, cleaving. . . . Accordingly, the feast of the leviathan will be an experience in which we will attain great connection to G-d and be roused with intense love to G-d. This is the feast of the leviathan.

A possible explanation as to the significance of the shor habar: *The prophet writes that the face of the ox in the Heavenly chariot is on the left side, alluding to the idea that the ox represents fear and dread, which stem from the left side [according to the kabbalah].*

It emerges that the leviathan represents love, while the shor habar *represents fear.*

The notion of a feast in which these two elements come together represents a synthesis of the two emotions of love

and fear together. The reality is that love and fear are the
antithesis of one another; when there is love, there's no
place for fear, and when there's fear, there's no place for
love. However, when it comes to serving G-d, they can come
together—love and fear in perfect synthesis.

TEXT B

Rabbi Levi Yitschak of Berditchev, Kedushat
Levi, *Beha'alotecha, s.v.* Mi yachileini basar

הקדוש ברוך הוא יעשה סעודה לעתיד לבא מלויתן ושור
הבר ובר אווזות ויין המשומר, כי באמת יאכלו בני ישראל
מן כאשר היה בימי יציאת מצרים (ראה חגיגה יב ע"ב),
לכך יעשה הקדוש ברוך הוא סעודת הצדיקים לעתיד
לבא מהדברים אלו, כדי שאחר זה כשיאכלו המן יטעמו
המאכלים שאכלו בסעודה [כי במן טועמים כל הטעמים
שרוצים לטעום בו, באופן שמכירים אותו טעם מלפנים,
ע"ש] ...כאשר היה ביציאת מצרים.

G-d is destined to make a feast from the leviathan, the
shor habar, *wild geese, and reserve wine. The truth is that*
the Jewish people will actually eat the manna as they did
when they left Egypt. So G-d makes a meal prior from these
delicacies, so that afterward, when they eat the manna, it
will assume the tastes from that meal [for the manna is able
to assume any taste wished upon it, a taste one has tasted
prior] . . . just as it was during the Exodus from Egypt.

Rabbi Levi Yitschak of Berditchev,
Kedushat Levi, Likutim

סעודה גדולה הוא שכר טוב לישראל מה שאכלו משום
מצות הבורא עליהם, והיינו סעודות שבת ויום טוב
והכנסת אורחים.

This great feast is a reward for the Jewish people who ate
food only to fulfill a mitzvah from G-d, namely the meals of
Shabbat, the festivals, and feeding guests.

Rabbi Isaiah Halevi ben Abraham Horowitz,
Shenei Luchot Haberit, Shaar Ha'otiyot, Kedushat
Ha'achilah §15

מצאתי בספר טעמי מצוה שחיבר הרב רבי מנחם הבבלי,
שכתב בלאו שלא לשתות יין נסך, וזה לשונו, ובימי חרפי
ראיתי אנשי מעשה שהיו מחמירים על עצמם, בראיית
הגוי היין לא היו רוצים לשתותו אע"פ שלא נגע בו הערל,
כיון שנתן עיניו בו אין בו סימן ברכה, ומנהג ותיקין הוא,
כיון שהערל רואה גוון היין או ריחו נתאוה לו במחשבתו,
וסתם מחשבת נוכרי לעבודה זרה, אם כן אע"פ שהוא ביד
ישראל כבר ציירו בשכלו, ואל תתמה על דקדוק החומרא
בכל שהוא, שהנשמר ממנו זוכה ליין המשומר בענביו אחר
שמשמח אלהים ואנשים בברכות, ותמה אני על המקילים
בארצות הערלים וכו'.

*I found in the book of mitzvah reasons composed by Rabbi
Menachem the Babylonian the following words [with regard
to the prohibition not to drink yayin nesech]:*

*I have observed scrupulous people who no longer drink wine
already from when a non-Jew only sees it, but doesn't neces-*

Rabbi Yeshayahu Halevi Horowitz (*Shalah*), 1565–1630

Kabbalist and author. Rabbi Horowitz was born in Prague and served
as rabbi in several prominent Jewish communities, including Frankfurt
am Main and his native Prague. After the passing of his wife in 1620, he
moved to Israel. In Tiberias, he completed his *Shenei Luchot Haberit*, an
encyclopedic compilation of kabbalistic ideas. He is buried in Tiberias, next
to Maimonides.

sarily touch it, arguing that from the moment the non-Jew gazes upon it, it no longer brings blessing.

This is a laudable custom, for when the non-Jew sees the rich color of the wine, or smells its pungent odor, he is drawn to it, and we can assume that he wishes to use it for idolatrous purposes. So though the wine is still in the Jew's hands, it is now in the non-Jew's imagination.

Do not question such scrupulousness that might seem tenuous, for one who is careful with such matters merits the yayin hameshumar *of which the Talmud speaks. I am indeed surprised by those who live among non-Jews and are not careful with this matter.*

The Jewish Learning Multiplex

Brought to you by the Rohr Jewish Learning Institute

In fulfillment of the Mandate of the Lubavitcher Rebbe, of blessed memory, whose leadership guides every step of our work, the mission of the Rohr Jewish Learning Institute is to transform Jewish life and the greater community through the study of Torah, connecting each Jew to our shared heritage of Jewish learning.

While our flagship program remains the cornerstone of our organization, JLI is proud to feature additional divisions catering to specific populations, in order to meet a wide array of educational needs.

Torah Studies provides a rich and nuanced encounter with the weekly Torah reading.

MyShiur courses are designed to assist students in developing the skills needed to study Talmud independently.

This rigorous fellowship program invites select college students to explore the fundamentals of Judaism.

Jewish teens forge their identity as they engage in Torah study, social interaction, and serious fun.

The **Rosh Chodesh Society** gathers Jewish women together once a month for intensive textual study.

TorahCafe.com provides an exclusive selection of top-rated Jewish educational videos.

This yearly event rejuvenates mind, body, and spirit with a powerful synthesis of Jewish learning and community.

Participants delve into our nation's past while exploring the Holy Land's relevance and meaning today.

Select affiliates are invited to partner with peers and noted professionals, as leaders of innovation and excellence.

Machon Shmuel is an institute providing Torah research in the service of educators worldwide.

Inasmuch as the development of these classes is ongoing, please note that some of the subjects, as well as the exact number of classes, are subject to change.